ISBN 978-1-4478-8499-6

© Caledonian Therapy Academy 2010
© Caledonian Therapy Academy 2011

Author: Louise Prunty

Front cover picture © Valua Vitaly – Istock Photo

Dedication:

To my employees, who are also my friends and always give me their support in my projects.

Join US on FACEBOOK pages for Updates:
**Caledonian Therapy Academy**
**Myscara**
**Glam Lash**

# Single Lash Extension Manual - 2nd Edition

# Contents

Foreword ........................................................................................................................ 5

Introduction .................................................................................................................... 6

   Unit Outcomes: ......................................................................................................... 6

Single Eyelash Comparison ............................................................................................ 8

   Comparison Table .................................................................................................... 8

   Physical effect eyelash extensions have on the eye .............................................. 10

   Describe the structure of the hair and hair growth cycle ..................................... 11

      Hair Growth Cycle ............................................................................................... 12

   Products ................................................................................................................. 13

Eyelash Categories ....................................................................................................... 14

      Width: ................................................................................................................... 14

      Curls of Lash: ........................................................................................................ 15

Products & Equipment Needed .................................................................................... 16

Maintaining safe and effective methods of working: ................................................... 19

   Preparation of Work Area ...................................................................................... 21

Consult, Plan & Prepare for service with clients ......................................................... 22

Contraindication ........................................................................................................... 24

Human Eyelash Theory ................................................................................................. 29

   Achieving the desired look: .................................................................................... 30

   Choosing the Correct Lashes ................................................................................. 33

Consultation ................................................................................................................. 34

   CONFIDENTIAL CLIENT CONSULTATION - ............................................................. 36

Preparing Your Clients for a Patch Test ........................................................................ 38

   Contra- actions: ..................................................................................................... 38

   Book appointment: ................................................................................................ 38

Single Lashes: Step By Step Instructions for Application ............................................. 39

Removal: ....................................................................................................................... 48

Start lash extension prep and procedure if client is getting a fresh set on.  Maintenance ................................. 49

Trouble Shooting ................................................................................................................ 49

Maintenance / infill ............................................................................................................ 51

    Conclusion: ....................................................................................................................... 51

    Glam Lash – In a Flash! (CPD Course Material) ............................................................... 52

    Glam Lash in a Flash! Tools ............................................................................................. 54

Appendix 2: Cosmetic / Fashion False Lashes ................................................................... 61

    Introduction  Strip Lashes & Cluster Lashes ................................................................... 61

Appendix 3: Legislation ...................................................................................................... 62

CODE OF ETHICS – Example code of ethics ........................................................................ 90

Insurance Providers: ........................................................................................................... 92

Bibliography ........................................................................................................................ 93

# Foreword

This book is aimed at students studying for qualification in applying 'Single Eyelash' Semi - Single / Single Eyelash Extension Qualification. For both College and private training providers using any system of single eyelash extensions. This updated version also covers 'MYscara' Semi Permanent mascara treatment.

This manual related to modules:

ITCT Module UV30426 – Apply Individual Single Lashes (Level 3)
ITEC Module Unit 809 - Apply Individual Single Lashes (Level 3)
HABIA, City & Guilds, SVQ / NVQ  – B15 Apply Single Eyelash Extensions (Level 3)
BABTAC Eyelash Extension Knowledge  Requirements
BABTAC Semi Permanent Mascara Application Knowledge Requirements
Guild of Beauty Therapists Eyelash Extension Knowledge  Requirements
Associated Beauty Therapists Eyelash Extension Knowledge Requirements

Glam Lash ™ & MYscara are products from the multiple award winning Caledonian Therapy Academy ®.

They exist to fill a gap in the market. It aims to offer quality, safe and reasonably priced products and training for professional therapists.

Glam Lash found there was not a readily available lash extension manual to purchase. Course providers were looking for a generic manual applicable to all systems that could be used in their training.

© Inga Ivanova – iStock Photo

This book is aimed as a manual for use in professional training or as a refresher for trained therapists.

You should not attempt any procedure in this book if you have not had any hands on professional training in this treatment.

# Introduction: Glam Lash – Semi Permanent Eyelash Extensions

## Unit Outcomes:

On completion of this unit you will:

1. Be able to prepare for an individual
Single lash treatment

2. Be able to provide individual Single lash
treatments

### Service Times:

Full set of single eyelash extensions –
120 minutes

### Practical Criteria:

The following practical criteria outcomes in this unit that you must achieve competently:

**Outcome 1:**

a. Prepare yourself, client and work area for individual Single lash extension treatment
b. Use suitable consultation techniques to identify treatment objectives
c. Interpret and accurately record the results of tests carried out prior to treatments
d. Provide clear recommendations to the client
e. Select products, tools and equipment to suit client treatment needs

**Outcome 2:**

a. Communicate and behave in a professional manner
b. Follow health and safety working practices
c. Position yourself and client correctly throughout the treatment
d. Use products, tools, equipment and techniques to suit client's treatment needs
e. Complete the treatment to the satisfaction of the client
f. Record and evaluate the results of the treatment
g. Provide suitable aftercare advice

# What are Single Eyelash Extensions?

Single Eyelash extensions sometimes also referred to as Permanent Eyelash Extensions, Semi - Permanent or Individual Eyelash Extensions provide length and thickness to your natural eyelashes. Single eyelash extensions need to be applied professionally to blend with your natural eyelashes. Lashes can be worn for a special occasion or every day wear. You can opt for a natural look and feel or a full glam look.

Quality eyelash extensions are water resistant and can be worn while you shower, swim or exercise. You can choose to apply mascara to the tips of your lash extensions as long as its water based mascara. Eyelash extensions come in a full range of widths, lengths and curls to suit every hair type and are available in many colours.

Usually an eyelash application procedure takes about 120 minutes, depending on the number of extensions being applied. Eyelash extensions are individually applied to the natural eyelash, they last for 8 to 12 weeks, the average life of a natural eyelash. The lash extensions are curled to replicate the curvature of the natural lashes, flat at the base and fine at the tip. Special strong cyanoacrylate glue is used to attach the synthetic lash to the natural lashes. The adhesive dries on the lash and sealant applied. However flexi glues dry with a water resistant seal.

Single lash extensions are the fastest growing beauty treatment in the UK. Many celebrities opt for this type of extensions over strip lashes as they look very natural and last well.

Depending on where you are in the country depends on what price you can charge the average is £75 for a set. £40 for half set. Or some therapists charge per lash applied (anything between £1 - £2.50 per lash).

UCB ₇
197748

# Single Eyelash Comparison

The single eyelash extensions are made from a type synthetic material (a type of plastic). There are manufactured in such a way so they resemble the natural eyelash. Each individual synthetic eyelash is attached to each eyelash with strong cyanoacrylate based glue.

Due to the lash growth cycle clients lose their natural lashes and therefore the synthetic lash extension attached to it. Therefore infills on lashes need to be done every 2-3 weeks to replaces the lashes that have fallen out.   With regular infill's lashes can be worn up to 3 months.

## *Comparison Table*

What's the difference between cosmetic lashes & Single lashes?

| | Single Lashes | Cosmetic False Lashes |
|---|---|---|
| **Appearance** | Natural & soft, look and feel similar to your own lashes | Hard, inflexible & look obviously false |
| **Adhesion Quality** | Extremely strong – Single until loss of eyelash at end of cycle (Around 2 – 3 Months) | Weak – short life adhesive so very easy to lose. (Around 1 – 5 days wear) |
| **Number of Application** | About 15 - 70 individually applied dependent on the desired look & amount of natural lashes. | Lashes knotted together with a bulbous end / lashes on strip. |
| **Wearability** | Long life for care free everyday wear. Limited Maintenance needed (Infill recommended between applications) | Short lift span – not conducive to daily wear & tear. |
| **Comfortability** | Light & flexible, | Heavy, Hard & can be uncomfortable |
| **Duration of Wear** | Up to 12 weeks | 1 -5 days |

*Basic Structure and function of eye:*

## The Basic Anatomy of the Eye

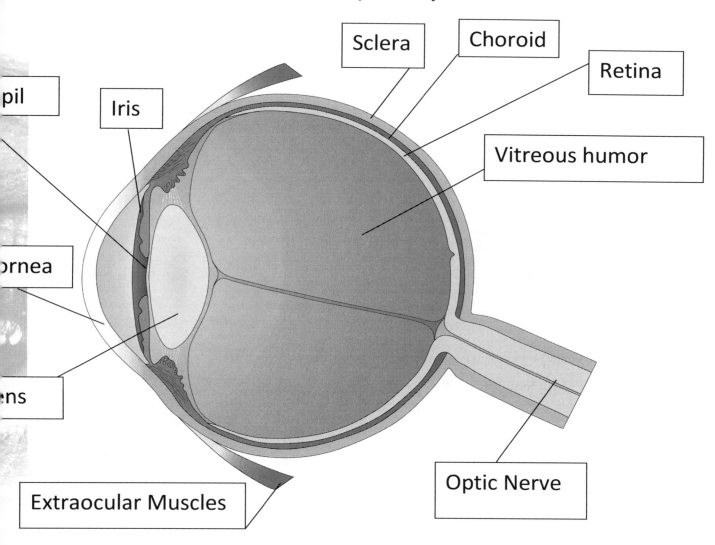

Sclera

Choroid

Retina

pil

Iris

Vitreous humor

ornea

ns

Extraocular Muscles

Optic Nerve

) David Gunn – iStock Photo

The eye is an extremely complex organ. The outermost layer of the eye is called the sclera (white of ye). Attached to the sclera are the muscles that move the eye, called the extraocular muscles. The clera maintains the shape of the eye. The front sixth of the sclera layer is clear and called the cornea. All light must first pass through the cornea when it enters the eye.

The second layer of the eye. It contains the blood vessels that supply blood to the structures of the eye. The front part of the choroids contains two structures: The ciliary body which is a muscular area that is

attached to the lens used for focusing. The iris (coloured part of the eye). People's iris colour can vary with the most common colours being blue or brown.

The innermost layer is called the retina which is the light sensing portion of the eye. The retina contains a chemical called rhodopsin which converts light into electrical impulses that the brain interprets as vision. The electrical impulses are carried by the optic nerve to the brain.

Inside the eyeball are two fluid filled sections the largest back section contains a clear jelly like material called vitreous humor. The smaller section contains a clear, watery material called aqueous humor. The aqueous humor is drained through the canal of Schlemm. In cases when this becomes blocked a disease called glaucoma usually develops. Covering the inside surface of the eyelids and sclera is a mucous membrane called conjunctiva.

The function of the eyelids is to protect the eye by blinking. Eyelashes and eyebrows protect the eye from particles such as dust that could injure or irritate the eye.

## *Physical effect eyelash extensions have on the eye*

**Over-stimulation of Meibomian Gland:**
The Meibomian gland is responsible for producing oil to lubricate the tear ducts. Over-simulation can occur due to using the incorrect lash length or thickness and wearing the extensions too long.

**Thickening of Cornea:** If eyes are closed for a long duration thickening of the cornea can occur which can cause blurred vision. This is a result of swelling behind the cornea. Once the eyes re-open the thickness reduces as normal vision returns.

# Describe the structure of the hair and hair growth cycle

## Hair Growth Cycle and Hair Structure

Hair structure:

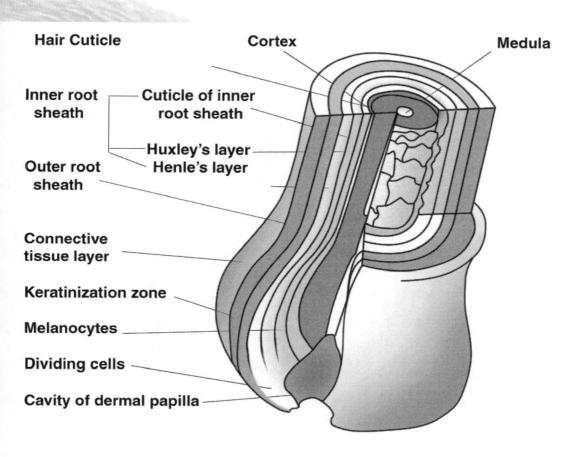

**Keratin:** A protein, which forms hair.
**Cuticle:** The hair cuticle is the outermost part of the hair shaft
**Cortex:** The middle layer of hair.
**Medulla:** The medulla is the inner most layer of the hair shaft.
**Inner Root Sheath:** The inner root sheath of the hair follicle is located between the outer root sheath and the hair shaft. It is made of three layers: Henle's layer, Huxley's layer, and the cuticle.
**Outer Root Sheath:** The outer root sheath of the hair follicle encloses the inner root sheath and hair shaft

**Connective Tissue:** Connective tissue is a form of fibrous tissue. Collagen is the main protein of connective tissue.

**Dermal Papillae:** The dermal papillae nourishes all hair follicles and bring food and oxygen to the lower layers of epidermal cells.

## Hair Growth Cycle

Eyelashes go through three stages of hair growth:

- Anagen (active/growth phase)

- Catagen (transition/regression phase) &

- Telogen (resting phase).

Unlike hair, eyelashes and eyebrows have a very short anagen phase of about 30-45 days. The short duration of eyelash growth stage explains why they are shorter than scalp hair.

Approximately 60-80% of the eyelashes are in this phase.

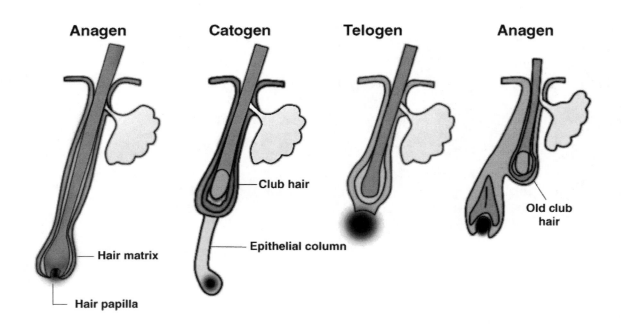

# Products

## Adhesive / Glue

Cyanoacrylate is the generic name for cyanoacrylate based fast-acting strong adhesives. Both main types of glues are cyanoacrylate based. Different manufacturer's glues may vary in setting time or bond strength. Flexible Glue is a rubber toughened single eyelash extension adhesive. Designed for professional technicians. Flexible Glue is one of the highest graded adhesives on the market, the performance is excellent.

© Glam Lash

The new rubber type toughened component gives extra strength, flexibility, quick set, increasing both the bonding time and longevity. Flexible glue glides on smoothly encapsulating each lash in a rubber seal. No solvents are used in the manufacture of the glue solvents are the ingredients that irritate the mucus membrane of the eye). Non flexible glue has been traditionally used in lash extensions some companies only offer this type of glue.

## Glue Comparison

| Flexible Glue Black | Non Flexible Glue Black or Clear |
|---|---|
| Odourless or Low Odour Self seal – no extra sealant needed Drying – Under 10 Seconds Bond Time 48 Hours | Odourless or Low Odour Sealant Required Drying – Between 10 - 20 Seconds Bond Time 48 Hours |
| Adhesive Specification: Professional use only | Adhesive Specification: Professional use only |
| Black Non-clumping with a Flexible seal Water proof 6 month shelf life Storage Keep cool (dark place) | Black or Clear  Not water proof sealant required Average 6 months shelf life Storage Keep cool (dark place) |

# Eyelash Categories

© *Glam Lash*

**Lashes**: Single eyelash extensions are synthetic lashes. Lash pots usually contain a 0.5g of lashes. Some companies offer smaller pots of 0.3g and larger 1g pots.

Please follow the sizing details below:

## Length:

Extra Short  = 3mm – 5mm (For lower lash extensions)

Short   = 6mm & 8mm (For end Lashes)

Medium  =  9mm - 12mm (Middle Lashes)

Long   = 13mm + (For Special occasions & Point use)

## Width:

0.10mm (Very fine – For application to very fine natural lashes)

0.15mm (Fine – For application to fine natural lashes)

0.20mm (Natural Volume – Most popular width, suits most people)

0.25mm (Thick -  Creates very noticeable lashes) * May be too heavy for some clients

0.3mm (Extra Thick – For false lash effect) * May be too heavy for most clients , however good for Point use.

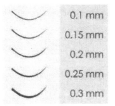

## Curls of Lash:

J – Natural Curl (Similar to the average curl of natural lash)

B – Slightly curlier than natural curl (Similar curl to using eyelash curlers)

C – Fairly curlier than natural curl (Similar to the effect of perming)

D – Very curly (False lash curl effect)

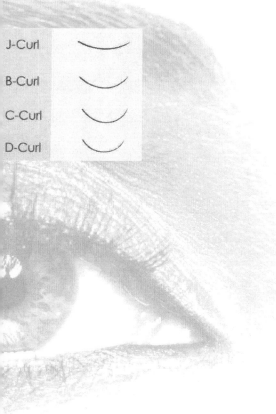

J-Curl

B-Curl

C-Curl

D-Curl

Note: Familiarise yourself with lash curls, thickness and length. Experiment with different types until its second nature in making lash choices.

Many companies will offer sample packs of lashes.

*All lash curls, thickness, lengths available at* **www.glamlash.co.uk**

## Products & Equipment Needed

Couch, Trolley, Stool & Mag Lamp:
**Couch** which is adjustable so client can lay flat or sit up.
**Trolley** which is large enough so set out your products on.
**Stool** which is height adjustable so you can get into the correct position for the treatment.
**Magnifying Lamp** (Mag Lamp):
To magnify the lashes and produce more light to make application easier.

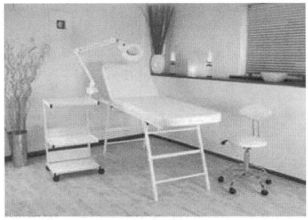

*House of Famuir Ltd ©*

You will also require ...

**Towels**
**Blanket**
**Additional support if appropriate**
**Headband**
**Bedroll**
**Tissues**
**Cotton wool**
**Mirror**

**Hand Sanitizer: Spray solution or gel to be used as and when required.**

*iStock Photo- ©*
*Juan Monino*

16

| Sterilising equipment: | Chemical sterilisation solution & Chemical immersion container or one of the following. UV cabinet , Autoclave, Hot bead steriliser. |
|---|---|
| Personal Protective | Uniform, mask or gloves if required. |
| Waste disposal Equipment | Means of disposing of materials safely. Local authorities may deal with commercial waste disposable or a private contractor maybe required. |

| | |
|---|---|
| Micro brushes: For precision application of primer and also used in the removal process. | |
| Adhesive cup and holder or Glue Stone: Both hold adhesive. Glue ring can make application faster as it is already on the hand. Glue stone keeps adhesive cool and usable for longer. | |
| Tweezers: I type or X type tweezers. Personal preference as to which type of tweezer is used. I type close when squeezed and open when released, X type open when squeezed and close when released. | |

Sealant (if required): Not every lash system will require the use of sealant. Flexible glue will not use sealer as when the glue dries it will produced its own water tight seal. Most other cyanoacrylate glue will require a sealant, always refer to manufacturer's instructions.

*Saline solution:* *Available in emergency pods or bottle to be used with eye bath. To use in the event of products getting into eye. Wash out immediately and seek medical advice.*

**Disposable mascara wands**
**Disposable face mask**
**Adhesives (clear/black)**
**Hypoallergenic transparent perforated plastic surgical tape**

**Eye Patches & Microporous Tape:** *Soothing and Lint free are recommended. Lint patches are not recommended as the lint fibres can get stuck to the glue and lashes. Micro pore tape can be used as an alternative to eye patches / eye pads.*

**Debonder / Adhesive Remover**
Liquid remover removes lashes rapidly and without any irritation or stinging to the eyes. Also comes as a gel remover.

**Make up Remover -**
Oil free make up remover, removes make up without leaving any oily residue.
Oil free is used as oil weakens the glue bond.

**Primer / Protein Remover** – Primes the natural lash ready for application.
Dehydrates lashes, removes remaining traces of oil / protein.

# Maintaining safe and effective methods of working:

A: Make sure you are complying with legislation from government and industry requirements.

B: Set up your working area so that it meets hygiene requirements and is suitable for the lash extension treatment to be carried out.

C: Ensure you are using personal protective equipment as required.

D: Ensure personal hygiene and appearance meets industry and company standards.

E: Ensure your hands are washed and a sanitising spray or gel is used prior to the treatment.

F: Ensure all equipment is cleaned and steralised to meet legislative and industry requirements. Also that disposable tools are disposed of after each client.

G: Position yourself and equipment so that they can be safely reached.

H: Ensure your own posture is correct to minimise fatigue and potential injury to yourself. Make use of adjustable equipment.

Maintain the client's privacy and modesty at all times.

: Maintain industry safety and hygiene practices throughout the treatment.

K: Dispose of materials safely and in a way that complies to legislative and local authority requirements.

L: Ensure that the service is cost effective, waste is limited and can be completed in an industry acceptable time.

M: Leave the working area in a safe, hygienic and in clean condition suitable for further services by yourself or another therapist.

N: Ensure client records are accurate, signed and stored securely and complying to legislative requirements.

# Preparation of Therapist

Have a high standard of personal hygiene.

Make sure you have fresh breath particularly after eating or if you smoke. Make sure hands smell fresh especially if you smoke.

A face mask can be worn for hygiene reasons

Wash hands before and after each client using anti-bacterial cleanser / soap and use hand sanitiser when required.

*iStock Photo* - © Catherine Yeulet

Wear flat comfortable shoes

Wear a clean and ironed uniform

Make sure Jewellery is removed with the exception of a plain wedding band and small stud earrings are acceptable to wear.

Make up if worn should be applied correctly and achieve a natural look.

Keep nails short, polish free and avoid artificial nails.

Long hair should tied or clipped back.

Make sure you are mentally prepared to carry out treatment. Smile and conduct in a friendly and polite manner.

# Preparation of Work Area

Make sure your working area is kept clean and tidy. Tidy up and clean after each client. The room should be ready before the client is taken into the room for treatment.

Make sure the treatment couch is set up ready for your client.

The couch should be cleaned and disinfected using surgical spirits or similar solution.

A couch cover applied, a fresh large towel laid down, couch roll to cover the couch. Small towel to cover clients chest and a pillow in pillow case should be laid out.

Ensure all equipment has been properly cleaned and sterilised prior to carrying out the treatment using UV Cabinet, barbacide (or similar), and is thoroughly cleaned following the treatment.

Micro brushes & disposable mascara wands should only be used once.

Do not put unused false lashes back into the pots once they have been used or removed they should be disposed of.

If adhesive, or adhesive remover, runs into the eye, wash out immediately with an eyewash / eyewash pod or plain water if eyewash unavailable, and get the client to seek medical attention.

The room should be well ventilated and not too hot. If a room is too hot it will cause the adhesive to dry too quickly and cause problems with the application.

# Consult, Plan & Prepare for service with clients

A: Using consultation techniques in a polite manner to determine what the client wants from the treatment. Encourage clients to speak by using open questions and encourage clients to ask questions.

B: Ask clients the appropriate questions to identify if they have any contraindications. Question further if they don't give clear answers.

C: Record your client's responses to questions on your consultation sheet.

D: Obtain an informed signed consent form from the client prior to carrying out the treatment. Use industry standard forms or have a solicitor draft one.

E: Obtain an informed signed consent form, from a parent or guardian for any minor (Under 16 years) prior to the treatment.

F: Ensure the parent or guardian of a minor is physically present throughout the treatment.

G: Make sure the client is in a safe and comfortable position before their treatment commences. Ask the client to let you know if they become uncomfortable and wish to move. So that you can stop what you are doing to allow them to move.

H: Thoroughly examine the eye area and surrounding area to identify if there is anything that could affect the treatment. Sometimes contraindications may not become apparent until the eyes have been examined.

I: Perform a patch test by following manufacturer's instructions.

J: Take action in response to any contra-indications identified.

K: Inform the client if a positive patch test occurs you will not be able to carry out the treatment.

L: Base recommendations on the client consultation and observation of lashes. Agree with client the achievable look and

make sure they are happy to proceed. If they are not happy and you have tried to accommodate do not carry out the treatment as the client may not be happy with the look and ask to have them removed.

M: Select the correct products for the look required.

N: Ensure the client is clothes, skin and hair are as protected as possible.

P: Make sure clients eye area is cleansed and lashes primed ready for application.

D: Ensure bottom lashes are taped down or patches are used to ensure they are kept out of the way.

## Notes:

_____

_____

_____

_____

_____

_____

_____

_____

_____

_____

_____

_____

_____

_____

_____

_____

_____

_____

# Contraindication

© Tim McClean Photography – iStock Photo

**Contraindication:** This is a condition which makes a client unsuitable for treatment or restrict the treatment the client can have. The condition may be visible or may be revealed during your consultation with your client.

Please also consult the following table of both contra-indications and cautions.

| Contra-Indications & Special Care | Caution Required Prior to Treatment |
|---|---|
| **Weak eyelashes** | **Do not carry out treatment (recommend homecare with lash tonic, review after 2 months)** |
| **Positive reaction to patch test (Allergy). Patch test 24 hrs before procedure.** | **Do not carry out** |
| **Hordeola /Sty / Styes** | **Do not carry out** |
| **Cysts** | **Do not carry out** |
| **Blepharitis** | **Do not carry out** |
| **Cuts, abrasions & swelling in the immediate area** | **Do not carry out** |
| **Chemotherapy** | **Do not carry out** |
| **Recent Lash Service (Chemical services such as lash perming)** | **Do not carry out** |

| tra-Indications & Special Care | Caution Required Prior to Treatment |
|---|---|
| Eye infections such as conjunctivitis | Do not carry out |
| Disorder in or around the eye area | Do not carry out |
| Disease | Do not carry out |
| Inflammation of or around the eye | Do not carry out |
| ent operations around eyes, head and face car tissue in immediate area. | Do not carry out |
| Skin Trauma, cuts, burns etc.. | Do not carry out |
| Eye Syndrome | GP Referral |
| ery Eyes | Do not carry out |
| ersensitive Skin / eyes | Do not carry out |
| atitis | Do not carry out |
| tact lenses | Client to remove prior to application |
| fever / Rhinitis | Eyes may be watery – check client comfort |
| ecia | Do not carry out |
| hotillomania | Do not carry out |
| strophobia | Ensure they are not claustrophobic as they will not be able to open their eyes during treatment. |
| s Palsy or any condition that makes ing eyes difficult | Do not carry out |
| disease / disorder causing shaking, ching or erratic movements | Do not carry out |
| coma | GP Referral |
| t Chemotherapy | GP Referral |
| junctivitis | Do not carry out |

## Contraindications Explained

Contraindications requiring medical permission – in circumstances where medical permission can not be obtained clients must sign an informed consent form stating that the treatment and its effects have been fully explained to them and confirm that they are willing to proceed without permission from their GP

**Eyelash Weakness:**
Clients who have weak or broken lashes are unsuitable for treatment until lashes are stronger. Appling synthetic lashes to weak natural lashes can cause further damage. Advise clients to use a lash tonic until their lashes have recovered.

**Positive Reaction to Patch Test:**
Under no circumstances should lashes be applied if a client had a reaction to the patch test. This would cause the client suffering and would invalidate your insurance.

**Styes:**
Treatment should not be carried out until the condition has cleared up, as carrying out the treatment would cause discomfort and irritation.

**Cysts**: Treatment should not be carried out as would cause discomfort.

**Blepharitis:** Is an ocular condition characterized by chronic inflammation of the eyelid, the severity and time course of which can vary

**Abrasions or Swelling:**
Any treatment in or around the area of abrasion / swelling could aggravate or worsen the condition.

**Chemotherapy:** Lashes weakened by chemotherapy, do not carry out lash extensions on someone who is being treated with Chemotherapy.

**Recent Lash Service:** 48 Hours should be left between lash services, for example having a lash perm and having lash extensions.

**Eye infections:**

For example, Conjunctivitis.

Conjunctivitis: It is an infection of the conjucntiva (the outer most layer of the eye that covers the sclera). The three most common types of conjunctivitis are: viral, allergic and bacterial. With the exception of the allergic type, conjunctivitis is highly contagious.

Viral Conjunctivitis

- Watery discharge, irritation, red eye, infection may begin in one eye and spread easily to the other eye.

Allergic Conjunctivitis

- Usually affects both eyes and causes itching and swollen eye lids.

Bacterial Conjunctivitis

- Discharge that may cause the eyelids to stick together, especially after sleeping
- Swelling of the conjunctiva, redness and irritation and/or a gritty feeling
- Usually affects one eye but may spread easily to the other eye

**Skin Disorder or skin disease in or around the eye area:**

**Diseases & Disorders of Hair**

**Folliculitis:** Folliculitis is the inflammation of one or more hair follicles. The condition may occur anywhere on the skin.

**Ingrown hairs:** Ingrown hair is a condition where the hair curls back or grows sideways into the skin.

**Hypertrichosis:** Hypertrichosis describes hair growth on the body in an amount considered abnormal.

**Pseudo folliculitis:** Curly hair tends to curl into the skin instead of straight out the follicle, leading to an inflammation reaction. It can make the skin look itchy and red.

**Any Inflammation of or around the eye:** Avoid lash extensions until inflammation has cleared.

**Recent operations around eyes, head and face or scar tissue in the immediate area:**

**Any skin trauma, cuts, burns etc.** Would cause discomfort, also risk of infection. Avoid lash extension until the condition has cleared up.

**Dry Eye Syndrome:** This occurs when the tear glands produce fewer tears. The symptoms range from mild irritation and a sensation of something in the eye, to severe discomfort such as burning. A GP referral is required prior to carrying out the treatment on a client.

**Watery Eyes:** Clients with watery eyes are not suitable for extensions, the watering of the eyes wouldn't allow the glue to set.

**Hypersensitive Skin / eyes:** Eyes may water and skin / eyes become irritated or sensitive avoid lash extensions.

**Keratitis:** An inflammation or infection of the cornea.

**Contact lenses:** Contact lenses need to be removed before treatment. Ask your client to bring their lens case and solution with them for their appointment.

**Hayfever / Rhinitis:** Can cause watery eyes, clients may also tend to rub their eyes. Check with client how severe their rhinitis is before carrying out treatment.

**Alopecia:** The medical description of the loss of hair from the head or body, sometimes to the extent of baldness. Some people may have alopecia of eyelashes.

**Trichotillomania:** The compulsive urge to pull out one's own hair is recognised as a disorder leading to noticeable hair loss, distress, and social or functional impairment.

**Claustrophobia:** If a client is claustrophobic they may not be able to have you in close proximity to them and or have their eyes closed for a long period of time. Most people with this condition are not suitable for lash extensions.

**Bells Palsy** or any condition that makes closing eyes difficult

**Twitching**: Any disease or disorder causing shaking, twitching or erratic movements. It would be virtually impossible to apply lashes to someone who twitches or shakes, it would also be very dangerous to the client.

**Glaucoma:** Glaucoma is a disease in which the optic nerve is damaged, leading to progressive, irreversible loss of vision.

**Post Chemotherapy:** For 6 months after chemotherapy lash extensions should not be applied.

# Human Eyelash Theory

The human eyelash grows between 6-9mm in length and they are located in distinct rows on the eyelid. Some people can have as little as 30 lashes on their upper lid, and others more than 150 lashes on the upper eyelid and about 80 eyelashes on the lower eyelid. The eyelashes in the upper eyelid are coarser and longer than the eyelashes on the lower eyelid.

The eyelash grows for approximately 30 days and then rests for the remainder of its life. An average life span of the eyelash is approximately 3 months.

For the purpose of eyelash extension application the eyelashes are split into three categories:

### 1: Premature
The premature eyelash is relatively new growth. These eyelashes are very short and weak and not yet strong enough to carry an eyelash extension.

### 2. Healthy
The healthy eyelash has been growing for 2-4 weeks and is now strong enough to carry an eyelash extension throughout its life. It is these eyelashes we look for when choosing donor eyelashes for an application.

### 3: Mature
These are the long lashes that are fully grown and could be prone to falling out at any time. Lash extensions can be applied to mature lashes but are likely to fall out soon after application.

## Achieving the desired look:

The look that can be achieved depends on various factors.

1: The client's natural eyelash length
2: Amount of donor lashes they have.
3: Product suitability
4: Condition of natural lash
5: Client preference
6: Positioning of eyes
7: Eye size & shape

**Clients Natural Lash Length:** Client can only have their natural lashes extended to 1/3 maximum. Therefore the look achieved is limited to the natural length of the lash.

**Amount of donor lashes:** 1 synthetic lash can be attached to 1 natural lash. Therefore the look achieved is limited to the amount of natural lashes a client has. If a client only has 30 donor lashes they will only be able to achieve a natural look.

**Product Suitability:** Lashes are chosen to suit the client. Synthetic lashes should follow a similar curvature to the natural lash. Certain lashes may not be appropriate to older clients. As we get older lashes get thinner and sparser therefore a thick, long lash look probably wouldn't suit an older client. Grey, brown, red and a variety of other lash colours can also be purchased to give clients the choice of lashes that will suit their hair or skin colouring.

**Condition of natural lash:** If the natural lash is not in prime condition it will affect the durability of the lash extensions.

**Client preference:** Clients have their own likes and dislikes, you might believe they would suit a natural look but your client might prefer a more noticeable look, your client's considerations and feedback should be taken into account.

# Positioning and size of eyes:

| Eye Shape | Corrective Steps |
|---|---|
| Close Set Eyes | Apply differing lengths of medium and longer lashes at the outside corners of the eyes and shorter ones on the insides. |
| Wide Set Eyes | Use medium lashes from the inner portion of the eye with longer in the centre and a mixture of shorter and medium on the outsides |
| Small Eyes | Use medium lashes from the inner portion of the eye with longer in the centre and a mixture of shorter and medium at the outside. |

*© McQueen Photography*

**Natural Look**

**Also Known**

**As...**

**Semi / Demi**

**Set**

**Or Half Set**

Total lash extensions 15 – 35 per Eye

For example: 7 Long, 9 Medium, 6 Short

However if a client has more lashes for

example 100 lashes on upper lid, 50 lashes

may be needed to achieve the look.

© Inga Ivanova – iStock Photo

***Glamorous /*** Total lash extensions 35+ per eye. As full
***Full Look*** as possible. Aim to attach a lash to all of
the natural lashes. Client with 35 lashes
example: 13 long, 16 Medium, 6 short.

Please note: There are general guidelines; you may need to add more or less lashes to keep the look symmetrical. The most common artificial lashes used are 9mm, 11mm & 13mm length on 0.2mm width.

The ***Natural Look*** should take approximately 1 – 1.5 hour to apply.
The ***Glamorous Look*** should take approximately 2  hours to apply.

## *Choosing the Correct Lashes*

Choosing the healthy donor lash will ensure longer lasting extensions. Mature lashes will tend to fall out first and will not have a very long life span when used for attaching lash extensions. Premature lashes will not have enough strength to hold up the lash extension. Your tutor will show you what a healthy donor lash should look like.

### Eyelash distribution

Dividing the eyelashes into sections will help you create the look the client desires.

Long - Section can be used for middle or outer sections.

Medium - Section can be used for inner middle or outer

Short - Section can be used for inner, outer, or both

Extra Short lashes usually only used for lower lash extensions

(this is taught on a separate course)

Health & Safety standards should always be as high as possible; you should still follow the guidelines noted to avoid any unnecessary problems.

> **Note: Safety precautions**
> 1. Any contra indications / Special care requirements should be noted on the client record cards, and procedures adhered to.
> 2. Caps and lids on bottles and jars should be immediately replaced when you have used them to avoid bacteria entering, contents drying out or spillage.
> 3. Only top lashes should be extended. Bottom lashes should not be extended until you have been trained

# Consultation

The aim of the consultation is to check for client suitability and to answer any of the client's questions and plan the treatment so that the client's requirements are met.

Consulting with client should take place in a comfortable relaxed area. You need to have good communication skills and ask a combination of open and closed questions when appropriate in the consultation process.

**Look for contra-indications**

Contractions that can occur:

Allergic reaction
Excessive erythema
Itching
Watery eyes
Inflammation
Infection
Client abuse i.e. rubbing / picking  or loss of natural lashes
Lower and upper lash adhesion
Foreign body enters clients eye i.e. lash/adhesive/dust

Depending on the severity of the contraction, in some cases you may need to use eye wash pods i.e. Saline eye irrigation procedure
Or refer client to their GP or A&E.

You will explain the features and benefits of the procedure at this stage including the application process.

Explain that the procedure requires the client to keep their eye closed for a long period – up to 2.5 hours. Some clients may not wish to do this and therefore will not be suitable for treatment.

The client must understand that the treatment is single and the permanence is dependent on the aftercare and life span of each eyelash.

Explain the types of 'look' which may be achieved with individual lashes and decide an effect based on the client's needs.

If the client wears contact lenses, they should be advised to bring their lenses container and solution with them so they can be removed prior to application.

The consultation is ideally carried out at least 24 hours prior to application as a patch test can be applied at this time.

A record card should be completed at this stage.

**Note:** If your client is not going to have a patch test make sure that your insurance provide covers not patch testing. At the time of printing there are several companies who do not require patch testing for Glam Lash Odourless glue.

## *CONFIDENTIAL CLIENT CONSULTATION -*

### SINGLE EYELASH EXTENSIONS

Client Name: ..................................................................................(Please circle) Male / Female

Address:

..........................................................................................................................................

.................................................Post Code...............................................Date of Birth.......................

Tel Landline: ...................................... Mobile: ......................................................

Email address:................................................................................................

Occupation: ...............................................................

Doctor's Name & Address:

...........................................................................................................................

...................................................................................................Tel: ...................................

**Contra-indications** (please circle all that apply)

**Medical Referal:**

Severe skin disorder,   Inflammation of Skin, Infectious skin diseases, Eye Disease, Eye Infections, Recent Eye Surgery, Blephartitis, Condition that causes shaking / jerking movements, Chemotherapy, Tricholotillomania,

**Restrict Service / Special care:**

Epilepsy,   Sensitive Skin,   Eye Surgery,   Skin Infections,   Eye Infections, Contact Lenses

Alopecia,  Watery Eyes,  Hayfever,  Asthma,  Allergies ..........................................

Are other conditions? ..............................................................................................

Are you currently taking any medication?

.............................................................................................

Any Other Relevant Information:

...........................................................................................................................

Have you had Eyelash Extensions before? Yes / No

**<u>For Therapist use only:</u>**

Patch Test completed: Yes / No Date and time of patch test.............................................................

Clients requirements:

...........................................................................................................................

Design Agreed: Partial / Natural / Glamorous / Infill

Lash Sizes used: 6mm / 7mm / 8mm / 9mm / 10mm / 11mm / 12mm / 13mm /14mm/15mm
Diameter 0.10mm / 0.15mm / 0.20mm / 0.25mm / 0.3mm

Colour(s) used: Black / Brown / Other

Diagram of applied lashes:

**Left**                                              **Right**

Disclaimer:

I confirm that to the best of my knowledge the answers I have given above are correct, and I have not withheld any information that may be relevant to my eyelash extension treatment. I agree that I am happy to receive the treatment outlined to me, agree to follow all advice and after care information provided for me.

Client Signature:
...................................................................Date:..........................................................

Therapist Signature:
......................................... ....................... Date: ...................................................

# Preparing Your Clients for a Patch Test

Some Insurance providers require that clients should have a patch test done at least 24 hours before the procedure. This can be done in the consultation stage. This is to ensure your client doesn't take a reaction to any products used, in particularly the adhesive.

1. Client to remove contact lenses / glasses if worn
2. Position the client comfortably
3. Client's neck should be supported by a pillow, additional supports can be used under client's knees to minimise back strain on the client.
4. Protect client's hair with headband or cap.
5. Protect client's upper body with towel or couch roll.
6. Wash your hands, apply sanitiser, put on protective gloves if using them.
7. Cleanse the eyes with an oil free cleaner
8. Brush through lashes
9. Tape clients bottom eyelashes down
10. Prime lashes
11. Place 2-3 lash extension on outer corner of both eyes. Lash extension adhesive must not touch the skin at any time.
12. Leave adhesive to dry for a few seconds.
13. Let client open eyes and let eyes get adjusted to the feel of the extensions.

*Contra- actions:* If a client complains of an uncomfortable feeling, stinging or eyes are excessively watery eyes, remove extensions immediately. Rinse eye with eye wash pod or eyebath with distilled water. Client to seek medical attention if discomfort continues.

*Book appointment:* Between now and the client returning for the appointment is a good time to get the lashes required for the appointment separated and laid out on a sponge or silicone lash stand. This will save time when the client comes back in to have the application carried out.

# Single Lashes: Step By Step Instructions for Application

Client must have had a patch test 24 hours prior to the treatment. Complete consultation and record card and set out necessary equipment and products.

© McQueen Photography – Glam Lash

1. Client to remove contact lenses / glasses if worn
2. Position the client comfortably
3. Client's neck should be supported by a pillow, additional supports can be used under client's knees to minimise back strain on the client.
4. Protect client's hair with headband or cap.
5. Protect client's upper body with towel or couch roll.
6. Wash your hands, apply sanitiser, put on protective gloves if using them.
7. Cleanse the eyes with an oil free cleaner

8. Assess the client for contraindications and decide which lashes to use

9. Lay out your lashes on the silicone pad.

10. Get clients to look up towards you then cover bottom lashes with micro-pore tape or eye patches. Client closes eyes (ensure lashes are lying correctly)

**Method 1: Patching lower lashes**

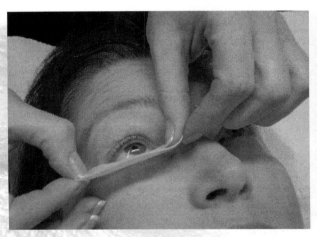

Remove patch from packet, peel of plastic backing. Apply at a 90 degree angle to the face initially then lay flat.

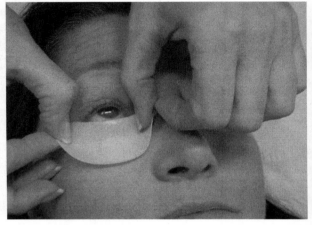

Secure pad at edges and smooth down under eyes.

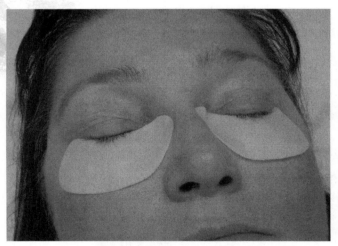

Patches covering all bottom lashes.

## Method 2: Taping down bottom lashes

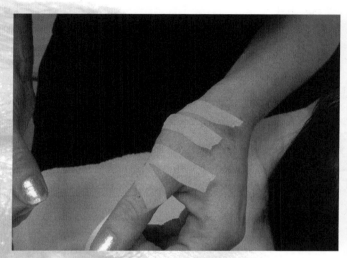

Tear off / cut tape from micropore roll.

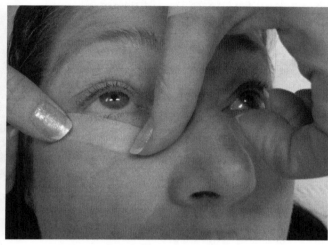

Tape down half of bottom lashes from outside corner.

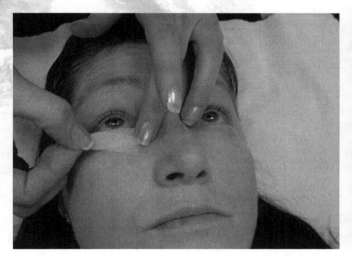

Use 2$^{nd}$ piece of tape to tape down bottom lashes from inside corner.

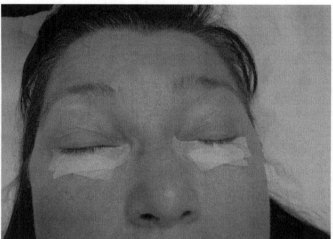

Repeat on other eye.

11. Let the client know their eyes must remain closed for the remainder of the treatment.

12. Check client is comfortable before proceeding.

13. Brush Lashes

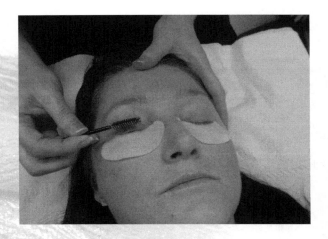

14. Prime lashes

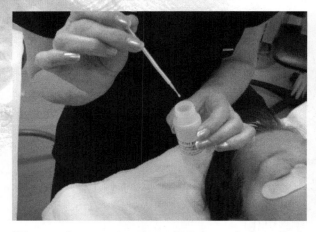
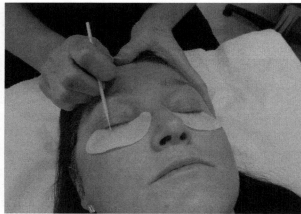

Dip a clean microbrush into primer. Dab off excess primer on couch roll or tissue.

Apply primer to every lash to remove all residue and oil.

15. Place glue on glue stone

16. Using I or X type tweezers pick up a lash extension (with right hand if you are right handed), dip 2/3 of extension into adhesive, using the curved tweezers or straight tweezers (with opposite hand) separate the natural lashes to find the donor lash

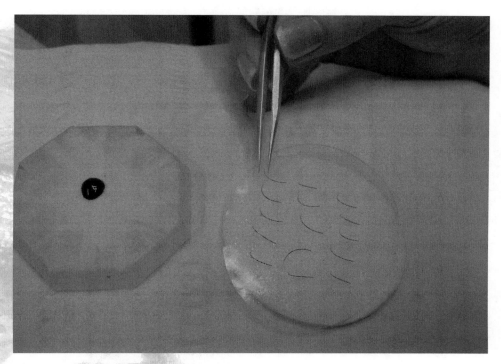

Glue on stone & lashes laid out

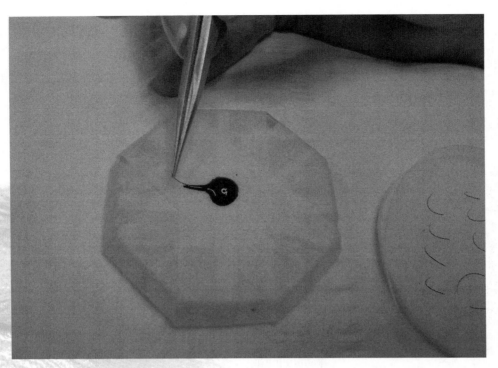

Pull lash through the glue leaving a 'tail' at the end so that excess glue and any air bubbles are removed, but still leaving enough glue on the lash.

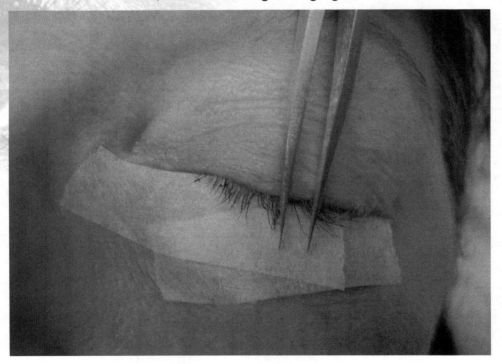

Isolating individual lash

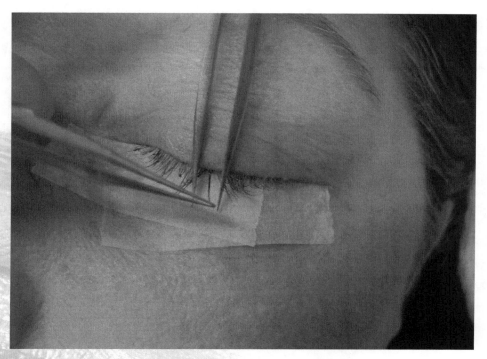

Synthetic single lash being applied to natural lash

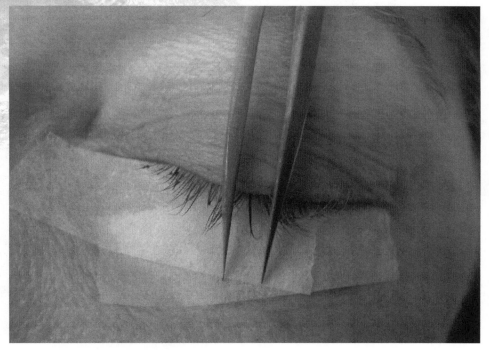

Result of lash being applied

17. Leave a 0.5mm - 1 mm space between the base of the lash extension and the eye lid and a 1-2 mm empty space at the inner and outer corner of both eyes to avoid irritation

18. Attach the lash extension to the selected healthy natural eyelash by using a back and forth motion 1-3 times until lashes are stuck together. Ensure the lash is applied correctly, pointing upwards and attached to the natural lash following its own shape.

19. Continue to apply lashes using the sequence described.

20. When the desired look is achieved carefully brush through the lashes

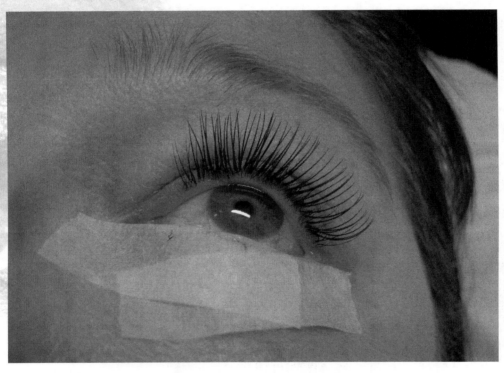

Final result

21. Apply sealant (unless using flexible glue)

22. When completed ask client to open her eyes and remove the tape from lower lashes (pulling from outward corner). Check results and offer client a mirror.

23. Discuss aftercare

24. Tidy and clean your working area

## After Care - Advise on how to take care of their lash extensions:

© Inga Ivanova – iStock Photo

**For the first 2 hours:**

Do not allow water to contact the eyelashes

**For the first 2 days:**

Do not wash eyes or lashes with hot water or steam the face.

Avoid swimming or exercise that can cause sweating.

**Thereafter....**

**Do not cover the eyelash area:** As it may cause eyelashes to curl, break and overlap each other.

**Avoid sleeping on your lashes.** This can bend the natural and synthetic lash. Use a clean mascara wand to carefully brush through lashes each morning to avoid tangling.

**Avoid Rubbing eyes as lashes**: This can loosen with persistent rubbing and can become uncomfortable.

**Avoid heat treatments:**

Jacuzzi or steam bath/sauna and tanning beds.

**Use only water soluble mascara:**

Do not apply mascara on adhesive area as mascara remover will weaken the bonding of the lash extension procedure.

**Do not use eye make up remover at all on lashes:**

This can cause the lash extension adhesive and extended lashes to weaken and fall out.

If a client has to use one, an oil free one and avoid lash area as much as possible.

Do not use any products near the eyes that contain oil:

Example: Moisturiser, eye cream etc..

**Do not attempt to put out lashes:** Pulling out the synthetic lash will also pull out the natural lash.

**Advise clients that lashes should be infilled approx every 2-3 weeks.**

## Removal:

Tools you will need for removal are:

Micro Brushes / cotton buds, tweezers & micropore tape.

- Clients eyes should always be closed for removal procedure

1. Place damp ½ cotton pads under each eye
2. Place 1 drop of remover onto the micro brush, do not saturate
3. Place the micro brush (with remover on) on top of the lash extension you wish to remove
4. Place the dry micro brush / cotton swab below the lash extension you wish to remove
5. Wedge the extension between the micro brushes and stroke along the lash, after a few strokes the lash extension will come off easily
6. If you are only removing one or two lash extensions be careful not to contaminate neighbouring lashes with remover as the bond will be compromised.
7. Do not allow any remover to enter client's eyes – damp cotton pad will absorb any excess remover.
8. One removal completed, cleanse eye area with oil free cleanser
9. Allow lashes to dry

**Start lash extension prep and procedure if client is getting a fresh set on.**

## Maintenance

1: Position the client on the couch

2: Check previous notes on treatment

3: Check over lashes

4: Wash and sanitise your hands

5: Prepare lashes as previously discussed with client

6: You may need to remove some single lashes that look out of place or untidy

7: Apply replacement lashes to comply with clients look they want to achieve this can take up to 45 minutes depending on look to achieve.

8: Show client their lashes

9: Recap aftercare advice

10. Rebook next appointment

11. Tidy & clean working area

## Notes:

_____
_____
_____
_____
_____
_____
_____
_____
_____

# Trouble Shooting

## Crossover lashes / drooping lashes

The lashes were applied too long for the natural lash. Lash extensions should be applied 1 third to half way along the donor lash size. If the lash falls over or crosses over the lash was too heavy for natural lash or not enough glue was applied.

## Lashes sticking together

Too much glue used or not allowing the glue enough time to dry when applying lashes.

## Lashes coming off

Not enough glue, wiping too much glue off, not rubbing lashes together 2 – 3 times during attachment. Have you cleansed using oil free cleanser and primed? Don't forget adhesive won't adhere to oil based products. Did you remove an adjacent lash and contaminate the other lash?

## Glue not coming out properly or too thin

Did you shake your glue before use? Make a hole in the bottle neck as adhesive may have hardened off in the bottle neck.

Always keep adhesives in a cool / dark area when not in use.

Always wipe the bottleneck and screw top back on well.

# Lash Rehabilitation

Clients that don't follow the correct aftercare risk damaging their lashes. When lashes are damaged or lost you can use products to encourage growth and condition. A lash tonic will promote growth and also improve condition of new lashes growing in. A lash conditioner will improve the condition and texture of the existing lashes. If clients have patches or missing lashes they should wait until their natural lashes have re-grown before having lash extensions on again.

# Maintenance / infill

We recommend that your client books an appointment for the first maintenance / infill session approx 2-3 weeks after the application. They should be charged for a half hours work and any lashes that have fallen out that make the eye unsymmetrical should be replaced.

The client should then attend regular maintenance sessions on a 3 week basis to keep the full look.

Keep a record on the client card where you originally placed lashes, if you cannot find enough 'healthy' lashes to adhere extensions to then finish off the application by attaching to mature lashes.

These will be the first to fall therefore will be the lashes you will replace on the first maintenance session.

The premature lashes will by now have grown into healthy lashes for you to attach the new extensions to. This cycle repeats month after month giving you a constant supply of healthy lashes to adhere to. A client could have the lash extension look they want on an on-going basis provided they attend regularly for infills.

## *Conclusion:*

With practical training and learning the contents of this manual you are on your way to becoming an excellent lash therapist. Enjoy! All products available at www.glamlash.co.uk

**Any questions relating to this manual please contact Caledonian Therapy Academy: Louise@ctacademy.co.uk**

## Appendix 1:

### *Glam Lash – In a Flash! (CPD Course Material)*

© Valua Vitaly – iStock Photo

**<u>Lash in a Flash! Workshops are half day workshops for trained lash technicians.</u>**

**By the end of your training you will be able to…**

Identify all tools & products used in the procedure

State the benefits of Glam Lash – In a Flash! extensions

Contra-indications of lash extensions

Fill in a client record card

Perform a patch test and assess the reaction

Prepare a client for lash extensions

Select correct lashes for the look your client wants to achieve

Carry out Semi Single Lash in a Flash! Lash Extension Procedure

Fill in case histories forms

## *Introduction*

It became apparent that there was a real need for a treatment that delivered a quick lash fix that still gave very similar results in terms of the finished look to single lash extensions. After much research and development we are proud to bring you: "Glam Lash in a Flash".

This new treatment has been designed to allow your clients to have beautiful lashes in 20 mins. Your clients will have the luxury of wearing "Lash in a Flash" for 2 weeks and then they will return to you for full removal. "Lash in a Flash" should only ever be worn by your client for a maximum of 2 weeks. Your client should always be advised they must return at 2 weeks for a complete removal. Any longer than 2 weeks and there is a risk of damage to the natural eyelash due to re -growth.

By using some of the skills you already have along with some new ones you will learn at your training session you will be able to produce beautiful sets of lashes in record time. This will enable you to service the needs of clients who would like to enjoy the finished results eyelash extensions produce without the 2 hour appointment.

### Glam Lash in a Flash! Tools

### Mink Eyelash Extensions

Mink eyelash extensions are individual, high gloss, soft, very flexible and curled to perfection. They are on a strip, pre sorted and are very easy to apply. They are available in a wide range of lengths, thicknesses and style of curl. This will allow you to offer your client anything from a very natural look up to a heavy more dramatic look.

### Tweezers

You can use either I type tweezers with a fine point or X type tweezers with a fine point. This is down to personal preference, some therapist prefer working with the clamp type mechanism of the X type whilst others prefer the more traditional straight tweezers. Either tweezers will deliver the same result in this treatment.

### Adhesive Finger Ring & Disposable Cups

Used during the application to allow the speedy application of the lash process. With disposable cups this is a very fast, easy & hygienic way to use the adhesive.

**The same primer, glue & remover that is used in the Glam Lash course are also used with Lash in a Flash.**

**All products available at www.glamlash.co.uk or from your local distributor.**

# Step by Step Application – Lash in a Flash!

1: Prep client as normal: i.e Cleanse eye area, tape down lower lashes and prime.
* Prep same as single eyelash extension preparation.

2: Place approx 2" of double sided sticky tape to the back of your hand (not the hand you use to work your tweezers) and place on the very edge of the tape a small amount of each size of the mink lashes your have selected in size order, starting with the largest first.

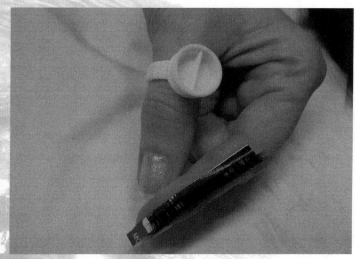

Glue ring and mink type lashes

3: Take your adhesive ring insert the cup and dispense your adhesive into the cup and place the ring into the thumb of the hand that you are not using to work your tweezers.

3: Starting with the longest extension dip this extension approx, 2/3's into the glue ring and working from the outside corner inwards place between 12 - 15 foundation lashes at 3- 4mm intervals, remember not to isolate.

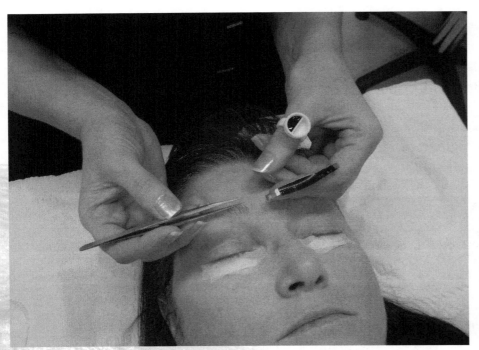

Picking off single lash from lash tape

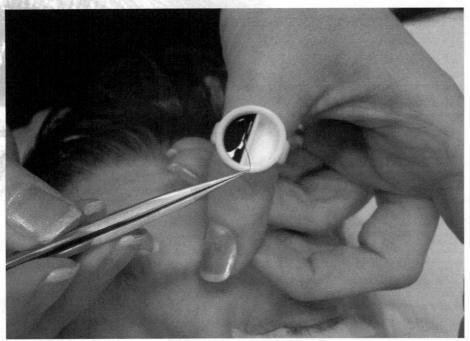

Dipping lash in glue – remove excess in the glue at the side of the ring

4: As you are working along the lash line gradually decrease
 your lash size according to your lash selection and design.

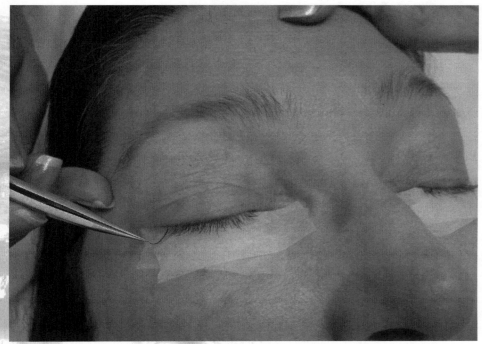

Applying lash

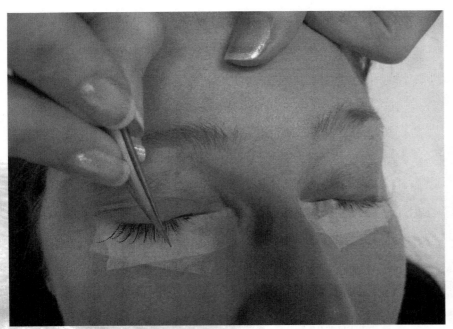

Applying foundation lashes

5: Once you have laid your "foundation lashes" go back to the first foundation lash on the outside corner and start to place lashes in between all the foundation lashes all the way along the lash line again decreasing in size as you work along towards the inner corner

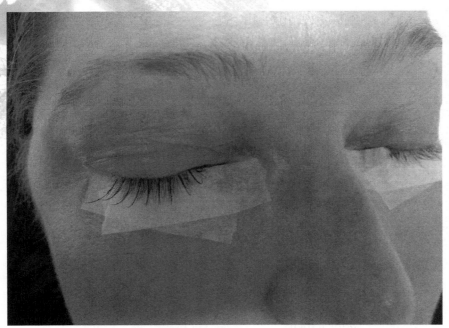

Foundation lashes applied

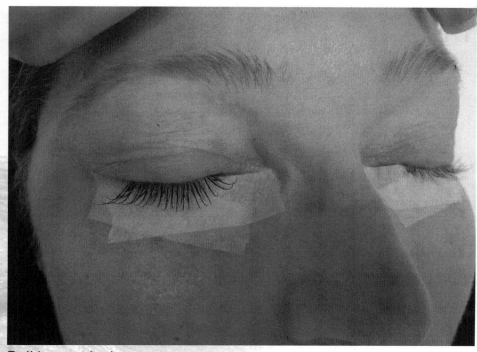

Bulking out lashes

6: Returning back to the outside corner once more using the foundation lashes as pillars to apply further extensions this will allow you to place the extensions in such away as to bulk out the lash line and allow for a fuller look.

7: Again decrease in size as you continue along the lash line towards the inner corner. You will have at the end of this stage up to 45 lashes on each eye. For an even fuller more dramatic look repeat this stage again.

It is Important to remember you MUST NOT brush the lashes through during or after application as there is no isolation of individual natural lashes so the lash extension will, in places, be attached to more than one natural lash. Brushing them through would be uncomfortable for your client and place a strain on the natural eyelashes. It is also important you advise your client as part of their aftercare not to brush them either.

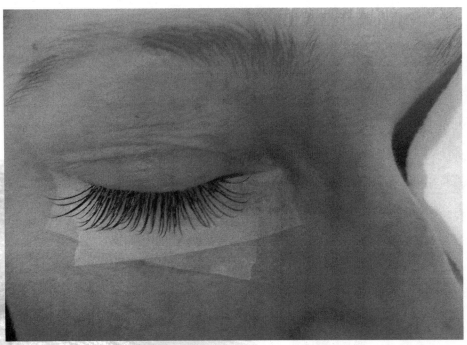

Final result

When you have the desired amount of lashes applied gently remove the under eye pad or tape from the lower lashes and ask your client to open her eyes slowly, if you have had strong lighting on please switch this off prior to asking your client to open their eyes as this could result in your clients eyes watering. Check the results and show your client in the mirror.

**Notes:**

_____

_____

_____

_____

_____

_____

_____

_____

_____

_____

# Appendix 2: Cosmetic / Fashion False Lashes

© coloroftime – iStock Photo

## *Introduction*

## *Strip Lashes*

## *Products / Tools need for application*

Strip Lashes - Half lashes or full strip
Eyelash glue – Cosmetic grade not Semi permanent / Single lash extension glue.
If you always wear black eyeliner then go for the black glue, if not opt for clear.
Tweezers
Liquid or gel eyeliner
Mascara

## *Application*

1: Use tweezers to gently remove the lashes from the packaging.
2: If you are using full strip lashes put them on the eye to measure and see how much you will need to trim off to fit.
3: Apply a thin layer of glue along the lash strip.

4: You can use tweezers to apply the lashes.
Hold the ends down first for 20 -30 seconds and move them along pressing it down as you go until you reach the other edge.
5: You can use a liquid eyeliner to blend the lash line.
6: Optional: Apply 2 coats of extension mascara to blend the natural and the cosmetic lashes.

# Appendix 3:
## *Reference Section : Legislation, Professionalism – Health and Safety*

### Legal framework

Insurance is required incase the worst ever happens and a client is injured and you are sued. Providing you are properly covered the insurance company would pay compensation to the client for their injuries. People in general are aware of their legal rights. Suing companies has become fairly common practice.

You will see many adverts in magazines for 'personal injury claims' on a no win no fee basis. In this day in age insurance is a must.

There are various insurance companies * See appendix at the back of manual.
Most professional associations provide their own insurance sometimes this is included in with the price of membership.

### Legislation

The law is made up of different types of Legislation Acts. A legislation act is a law laid down by government which must be adhered to. In recent years the law in the United Kingdom has been heavily influenced by the European Union (EU). The EU is working towards integrating the laws in its member EU states.

### Health and safety legislation

The law demands that every place of work is a safe place to be for employees and is extended to everyone who enters the premises. Health and safety legislation is part of criminal law. Failure to comply with the law has serious repercussions.

The main responsibilities for health and safety are with the employer.

An employer must have the appropriate health and safety policies in place.

The main ones are, the place of work is a safe environment and all staff are trained in health and safety procedures. All employers should have employers insurance as it's a statutory requirement. Also a Health & Safety poster must be displayed detailing the person responsible for health and safety.

**Health and Safety Executive**

The Health and Safety Executive (HSE) is the main authority on health and safety. The HSE provides information and gives advice through its area offices. It also enforces health and safety legislation by sending inspectors from the local authority to check up on companies standards of health and safety. These inspectors are usually Environmental Health

Officers. Every council has Environment Health Officers. There powers include the right to carry out an inspection of the premises or an investigation into a complaint. If the inspectors are not satisfied with the standards of health and safety, they will issue either an improvement notice or a prohibition notice.

An Improvement notice will allow the employer 21 days to make specified improvements an employer who fails to comply with the notice by the given date will probably end up in court. A Prohibition notice is far more serious. In this case the health and safety risk has been assessed as so severe that the business has been shut down by the officer until the improvements have been made. The business will not be allowed to start operating again until the Environmental protection officer has seen that you have dealt with all issues in their report. An inspector will come back to check compliance with the notice. Failure to comply with the notice can result in criminal prosecution.

## Fire Precautions Act (1971)

The Act furthers the provisions for the protection of persons from fire risks. If any premises are put to use a certificate is usually required from the fire authority. In certain circumstances the fire authority may grant exemption from the requirements to have a fire certificate, otherwise a copy of the fire certificate is sent to the occupier and it must be kept on the premises. The owner of the building is also sent a copy of the certificate.

It is an offence not to have or to have applied for a fire certificate for any designated premises. Contravention of any requirement imposed in a fire certificate is also an offence. A person guilty of an offence (with some exceptions) shall be liable to summary convictions to a fine or imprisonment or both.

## Health & Safety - First Aid Regulations (1981)

The Health and Safety (First-Aid) Regulations 1981 require employers to provide adequate and appropriate equipment, facilities and personnel to ensure their employees receive immediate attention if they are injured or taken ill at work. These Regulations apply to all workplaces including those with less than five employees and to the self-employed.

What is 'adequate and appropriate' will depend on the circumstances in the workplace. This includes whether trained first-aiders are needed, what should be included in a first-aid box and if a first-aid room is required. Employers should carry out an assessment of first-aid needs to determine what to provide.

The Regulations do not place a legal duty on employers to make first-aid provision for non-employees such as the public. However, HSE strongly recommends that non-employees are included in an assessment of first-aid needs and that provision is made for them.

## The Management of Health & Safety Regulations

Make sure you have a clear Health and Safety policy that all employees are familiar with. All employees must be committed to health and safety and realise their roll in keeping their environment safe.

- Assess the skills needed to carry out all tasks safely.
- Provide the means to ensure that all employees, including your managers, supervisors and temporary staff, are adequately instructed and trained.
- Ensure that people doing especially dangerous work have the necessary training, experience and other qualities to carry out the work safely.
- Arrange for access to sound advice and help.
- Carry out restructuring or reorganisation to ensure the competence of those taking on new health and safety responsibilities.
let everyone know health and safety is important.
- Ensure that managers, supervisors and team leaders understand their responsibilities and have the time and resources to carry them out.

## The Workplace (Health, Safety & Welfare) Regulations Requirements under these Regulations

Employers have a general duty under section 2 of the Health and Safety at Work Act 1974 to ensure, so far as is reasonably practicable, the health, safety and welfare of their employees at work. People in control of non-domestic premises have a duty (under section 4 of the Act) towards people who are not their employees but use their premises. The Regulations expand on these duties and are intended to protect the health and safety of everyone in the workplace, and ensure that adequate welfare facilities are provided for people at work.

These Regulations aim to ensure that workplaces meet the health, safety and welfare needs of all members of a workforce, including people with disabilities. Several of the Regulations require things to be 'suitable'. Regulation 2(3) makes it clear that things should be suitable for anyone. This includes people with disabilities. Where necessary, parts of the workplace, including in particular doors, passageways, stairs, showers, washbasins, lavatories and workstations, should be made accessible for disabled people.

## Health

The measures outlined in this section contribute to the general working environment of people in the workplace.

## Ventilation

Workplaces need to be adequately ventilated. Fresh, clean air should be drawn from a source outside the workplace, uncontaminated by discharges from flues, chimneys or other process outlets, and be circulated through the workrooms.

Ventilation should also remove and dilute warm, humid air and provide air movement, which gives a sense of freshness without causing a draught. If the workplace contains process or heating equipment or other sources of dust, fumes or vapours, more fresh air will be needed to provide adequate ventilation.

Windows or other openings may provide sufficient ventilation but, where necessary, mechanical ventilation systems should be provided and regularly maintained.

## Temperatures in indoor workplaces

Environmental factors (such as humidity and sources of heat in the workplace) combine with personal factors (such as the clothing a worker is wearing and how physically demanding their work is) to influence what is called someone's 'thermal comfort'.

Individual personal preference makes it difficult to specify a thermal environment which satisfies everyone. For workplaces where the activity is mainly sedentary, for example offices, the temperature should normally be at least 16 °C. If work involves physical effort it should be at least 13 °C (unless other laws require lower temperatures).

## Work in hot or cold environments

The risk to the health of workers increases as conditions move further away from those generally accepted as comfortable. Risk of heat stress arises, for example, from working in high air temperatures, exposure to high thermal radiation or high levels of humidity, such as those found in foundries, glass works and laundries. Cold stress may arise, for example, from working in cold stores, food preparation areas and in the open air during winter.

Assessment of the risk to workers' health from working in either a hot or cold environment needs to consider both personal and environmental factors. Personal factors include body activity, the amount and type of clothing, and duration of exposure. Environmental factors include ambient temperature and radiant heat; and if the work is outside, sunlight, wind velocity and the presence of rain or snow.

## Lighting

Lighting should be sufficient to enable people to work and move about safely. If necessary, local lighting should be provided at individual workstations and at places of particular risk such as crossing points on traffic routes. Lighting and light fittings should not create any hazard. Automatic emergency lighting, powered by an independent source, should be provided where sudden loss of light would create a risk.

## Cleanliness and waste materials

Every workplace and the furniture, furnishings and fittings should be kept clean and it should be possible to keep the surfaces of floors, walls and ceilings clean. Cleaning and the removal of waste should be carried out as necessary by an effective method. Waste should be stored in suitable receptacles.

## Room dimensions and space

Workrooms should have enough free space to allow people to move about with ease. The volume of the room when empty, divided by the number of people normally working in it, should be at least 11 cubic metres. All or part of a room over 3.0 m high should be counted as 3.0 m high. 11 cubic metres per person is a minimum and may be insufficient depending on the layout, contents and the nature of the work.

## Workstations and seating

Workstations should be suitable for the people using them and for the work they do. People should be able to leave workstations swiftly in an emergency. If work can or must be done sitting, seats which are suitable for the people using them and for the work they do should be provided. Seating should give adequate support for the lower back, and footrests should be provided for workers who cannot place their feet flat on the floor.

## Safety

### Maintenance

The workplace, and certain equipment, devices and systems should be maintained in efficient working order (efficient for health, safety and welfare). Such maintenance is required for mechanical ventilation systems; equipment and devices which would cause a risk to health, safety or welfare if a fault occurred; and equipment and devices intended to prevent or reduce hazard.

The condition of the buildings needs to be monitored to ensure that they have appropriate stability and solidity for their use. This includes risks from the normal running of the work process (eg vibration, floor loadings) and foreseeable risks (eg fire in a cylinder store).

## Floors and traffic routes

'Traffic route' means a route for pedestrian traffic, vehicles, or both, and includes any stairs, fixed ladder, doorway, gateway, loading bay or ramp.

There should be sufficient traffic routes, of sufficient width and headroom, to allow people and vehicles to circulate safely with ease. Horizontal swinging barriers used as gates at car park or similar entrances should be locked open or locked shut (preferably by padlock) so that they do not swing open and constitute a risk to oncoming vehicles. This guidance also relates to duties under the requirements of the Regulations covering doors and gates.

To allow people and vehicles to move safely, the best approach is to keep vehicles and pedestrians apart by ensuring that they use entirely separate routes. If people and vehicles have to share a traffic route, use kerbs, barriers or clear markings to designate a safe walkway and, where pedestrians need to cross a vehicle route, provide clearly marked crossing points with good visibility, bridges or subways. Make sure the shared route is well lit.

It is often difficult for drivers to see behind their vehicle when they are reversing; as far as possible, plan traffic routes so that drivers do not need to reverse. This can be achieved by using one-way systems and drive-through loading areas.

Set appropriate speed limits, and make sure they, and any other traffic rules, are obeyed.

Provide route markings and signs so that drivers and pedestrians know where to go and what rules apply to their route, so they are warned of any potential hazards.

Loading bays should have at least one exit point from the lower level, or a refuge should be provided to avoid people being struck or crushed by vehicles.

## Transparent or translucent doors, gates or walls and windows

Windows, transparent or translucent surfaces in walls, partitions, doors and gates should, where necessary for reasons of health and safety, be made of safety material or be protected against breakage. If there is a danger of people coming into contact with it, it should be marked or incorporate features to make it apparent.

Employers will need to consider whether there is a foreseeable risk of people coming into contact with glazing and being hurt. If this is the case, the glazing will need to meet the requirements of the Regulations.

69

**Windows**

Openable windows, skylights and ventilators should be capable of being opened, closed or adjusted safely and, when open, should not pose any undue risk to anyone.

Windows and skylights should be designed so that they may be cleaned safely. When considering if they can be cleaned safely, account may be taken of equipment used in conjunction with the window or skylight or of devices fitted to the building.

**Doors and gates**

Doors and gates should be suitably constructed and fitted with safety devices if necessary. Doors and gates which swing both ways and conventionally hinged doors on main traffic routes should have a transparent viewing panel.

Power-operated doors and gates should have safety features to prevent people being struck or trapped and, where necessary, should have a readily identifiable and accessible control switch or device so that they can be stopped quickly in an emergency.

Upward-opening doors or gates need to be fitted with an effective device to prevent them falling back. Provided that they are properly maintained, counterbalance springs and similar counterbalance or ratchet devices to hold them in the open position are acceptable. Powered vertical opening doors that are powerful enough to lift an adult or child should be fitted with measures to prevent this.

**Escalators and moving walkways**

Escalators and moving walkways should function safely, be equipped with any necessary safety devices, and be fitted with one or more emergency stop controls which are easily identifiable and readily accessible.

## Welfare

### Sanitary conveniences and washing facilities

Suitable and sufficient sanitary conveniences and washing facilities should be provided at readily accessible places. They and the rooms containing them should be kept clean and be adequately ventilated and lit. Washing facilities should have running hot and cold or warm water, soap and clean towels or other means of cleaning or drying. If required by the type of work, showers should also be provided. Men and women should have separate facilities unless each facility is in a separate room with a lockable door and is for use by only one person at a time.

### Drinking water

An adequate supply of high-quality drinking water, with an upward drinking jet or suitable cups, should be provided. Water should only be provided in refillable enclosed containers where it cannot be obtained directly from a mains supply. The containers should be refilled at least daily (unless they are chilled water dispensers where the containers are returned to the supplier for refilling). Bottled water/water dispensing systems may still be provided as a secondary source of drinking water. Drinking water does not have to be marked unless there is a significant risk of people drinking non-drinking water.

### Accommodation for clothing and facilities for changing

Adequate, suitable and secure space should be provided to store workers' own clothing and special clothing. As far as is reasonably practicable the facilities should allow for drying clothing. Changing facilities should also be provided for workers who change into special work clothing. The facilities should be readily accessible from workrooms and washing and eating facilities, and should ensure the privacy of the user, be of sufficient capacity, and be provided with seating.

## Facilities for rest and to eat meals

Suitable and sufficient, readily accessible rest facilities should be provided.

Seats should be provided for workers to use during breaks. These should be in a place where personal protective equipment need not be worn. Rest areas or rooms should be large enough and have sufficient seats with backrests and tables for the number of workers likely to use them at any one time, including suitable access and seating which is adequate for the number of disabled people at work.

Where workers regularly eat meals at work, suitable and sufficient facilities should be provided for the purpose. Such facilities should also be provided where food would otherwise be likely to be contaminated

Work areas can be counted as rest areas and as eating facilities, provided they are adequately clean and there is a suitable surface on which to place food.

Where provided, eating facilities should include a facility for preparing or obtaining a hot drink. Where hot food cannot be obtained in or reasonably near to the workplace, workers may need to be provided with a means for heating their own food (eg microwave oven).

Canteens or restaurants may be used as rest facilities provided there is no obligation to purchase food.

Suitable rest facilities should be provided for pregnant women and nursing mothers. They should be near to sanitary facilities and, where necessary, include the facility to lie down.

From 1 July 2007, it has been against the law to smoke in virtually all enclosed public places and workplaces in England, including most work vehicles. Similar legislation exists in Scotland and Wales.

## The Manual Handling Operations Regulations

### The MHOR Regulations in Brief

The employer's duty is to avoid Manual Handling as far as reasonably practicable if there is a possibility of injury. If this cannot be done then they must reduce the risk of injury as far as reasonably practicable. If an employee is complaining of discomfort, any changes to work to avoid or reduce manual handling must be monitored to check they are having a positive effect. However, if they are not working satisfactorily, alternatives must be considered.

The regulations set out a hierarchy of measures to reduce the risks of manual handling. These are in regulation 4(1) and as follows:

Avoid hazardous manual handling operations so far as reasonably practicable;

Assess any hazardous manual handling operations that cannot be avoided;

Reduce the risk of injury so far as reasonably practicable.

The guidance on the Manual Handling Regulations includes a risk assessment filter and checklist to help employers assess manual handling tasks. A revised version of the MHOR was published in March 2004. It also includes a checklist to help you assess the risk(s) posed by workplace pushing and pullling activities.

In addition, employees have duties to take reasonable care of their own health and safety and that of others who may be affected by their actions. They must communicate with their employers so that they too are able to meet their health and safety duties.

Employees have general health and safety duties to:
Follow appropriate systems of work laid down for their safety.
Make proper use of equipment provided for their safety.
Co-operate with their employer on health and safety matters.
Inform the employer if they identify hazardous handling activities.
Take care to ensure that their activities do not put others at risk.

## The Personal Protective Equipment at Work Regulations

Employers have basic duties concerning the provision and use of personal protective equipment (PPE) at work and this document, explains what you need to do to meet the requirements of the Personal Protective Equipment at Work Regulations 1992 (as amended).

### What is PPE?

PPE is defined in the Regulations as 'all equipment (including clothing affording protection against the weather) which is intended to be worn or held by a person at work and which protects him against one or more risks to his health or safety', eg safety helmets, gloves, eye protection, high visibility clothing, safety footwear and safety harnesses. What do the Regulations require?

The main requirement of the PPE at Work Regulations 1992 is that personal protective equipment is to be supplied and used at work wherever there are risks to health and safety that cannot be adequately controlled in other ways.
The Regulations also require that PPE:

- is properly assessed before use to ensure it is suitable;
- is maintained and stored properly;
- is provided with instructions on how to use it safely; and
- is used correctly by employees.

## Charging for PPE

An employer cannot ask for money from an employee for PPE, whether it is returnable or not. This includes agency workers if they are legally regarded as your employees. If employment has been terminated and the employee keeps the PPE without the employer's permission, then, as long as it has been made clear in the contract of employment, the employer may be able to deduct the cost of the replacement from any wages owed.

## The Provision and Use of Work Equipment Regulations

The Regulations require risks to people's health and safety, from equipment that they use at work, to be prevented or controlled. In addition to the requirements of PUWER, lifting equipment is also subject to the requirements of the Lifting Operations and Lifting Equipment Regulations 1998.

## What does PUWER do?

In general terms, the Regulations require that equipment provided for use at work is:
suitable for the intended use;
safe for use, maintained in a safe condition and, in certain circumstances, inspected to ensure this remains the case;
used only by people who have received adequate information, instruction and training; and
accompanied by suitable safety measures, eg protective devices, markings, warnings.

## What equipment is covered by the Regulations?

Generally, any equipment which is used by an employee at work is covered, for example hammers, knives, ladders, drilling machines, power presses, circular saws, photocopiers, lifting equipment (including lifts), dumper trucks and motor vehicles. Similarly, if you allow employees to provide their own equipment, it too will be covered by PUWER and you will need to make sure it complies.

**The Control of Substances Hazardous to Health Regulations (COSHH)**

COSHH is the law that requires employers to control substances that are hazardous to health[1]. You can prevent or reduce workers' exposure to hazardous substances by:

finding out what the health hazards are;

deciding how to prevent harm to health (risk assessment[2]);

providing control measures to reduce harm to health;

making sure they are used ;

keeping all control measures in good working order;

providing information, instruction and training for employees and others;

providing monitoring and health surveillance in appropriate cases;

planning for emergencies.

Most businesses use substances, or products that are mixtures of substances. Some processes create substances. These could cause harm to employees, contractors and other people.

Sometimes substances are easily recognised as harmful. Common substances such as paint, bleach or dust from natural materials may also be harmful.

COSHH covers chemicals, products containing chemicals, fumes, dusts, vapours, mists and gases, and biological agents (germs). If the packaging has any of the hazard symbols[1] then it is classed as a hazardous substance.

COSHH also covers asphyxiating gases.

**The Electricity at Work Regulations**

**What are the hazards?**

The main hazards are:

contact with live parts causing shock and burns (normal mains voltage,

230 volts AC, can kill);

faults which could cause fires;

fire or explosion where electricity could be the source of ignition in a potentially flammable or

explosive atmosphere, eg in a spray paint booth.

**Assessing the risk**

*Hazard* means anything which can cause harm.

*Risk* is the chance, great or small, that someone will actually be harmed by the hazard.

The first stage in controlling risk is to carry out a risk assessment in order to identify what needs

to be done. (This is a legal requirement for all risks at work.) Health and Safety Executive

Some items of equipment can also involve greater risk than others. Extension leads are particularly liable to damage - to their plugs and sockets, to their electrical connections, and to the cable itself. Other flexible leads, particularly those connected to equipment which is moved a great deal, can suffer from similar problems.

More information on carrying out risk assessments is available in other HSE publications listed on page 5 of this document.

**Reducing the risk**

Once you have completed the risk assessment, you can use your findings to reduce unacceptable risks from the electrical equipment in your place of work. There are many things you can do to achieve this; here are some.

*Ensure that the electrical installation is safe*

install new electrical systems to a suitable standard, eg BS 7671 Requirements for electrical installations, and then maintain them in a safe condition;

existing installations should also be properly maintained;

provide enough socket-outlets - overloading socket-outlets by using adaptors can cause fires.

*Provide safe and suitable equipment*

choose equipment that is suitable for its working environment;

electrical risks can sometimes be eliminated by using air, hydraulic or hand-powered tools. These are especially useful in harsh conditions;

- ensure that equipment is safe when supplied and then maintain it in a safe condition;
- provide an accessible and clearly identified switch near each fixed machine to cut off power in an emergency;
- for portable equipment, use socket-outlets which are close by so that equipment can be easily disconnected in an emergency;
- the ends of flexible cables should always have the outer sheath of the cable firmly clamped to stop the wires (particularly the earth) pulling out of the terminals;

- Do not use strip connector blocks covered in insulating tape;

some types of equipment are double insulated. These are often marked with a 'double-square' symbol . The supply leads have only two wires - live (brown) and neutral (blue). Make sure they are properly connected if the plug is not a moulded-on type;

protect lightbulbs and other equipment which could easily be damaged in use. There is a risk of electric shock if they are broken;

electrical equipment used in flammable/explosive atmospheres should be designed to stop it from causing ignition. You may need specialist advice.

## Reduce the voltage

One of the best ways of reducing the risk of injury when using electrical equipment is to limit the supply voltage to the lowest needed to get the job done, such as:

temporary lighting can be run at lower voltages, eg 12, 25, 50 or 110 volts;

where electrically powered tools are used, battery operated are safest;

portable tools are readily available which are designed to be run from a 110 volts centre-tapped-to-earth supply.

## Provide a safety device

If equipment operating at 230 volts or higher is used, an RCD (residual current device) can provide additional safety. An RCD is a device which detects some, but not all, faults in the electrical system and rapidly switches off the supply. The best place for an RCD is built into the main switchboard or the socket-outlet, as this means that the supply cables are Singlely protected. If this is not possible a plug incorporating an RCD, or a plug-in RCD adaptor, can also provide additional safety.

RCDs for protecting people have a rated tripping current (sensitivity) of not more than 30 milliamps (mA). Remember:

an RCD is a valuable safety device, never bypass it;

if the RCD trips, it is a sign there is a fault. Check the system before using it again;

if the RCD trips frequently and no fault can be found in the system, consult the manufacturer of the RCD; the RCD has a test button to check that its mechanism is free and functioning. Use this regularly.

### Carry out preventative maintenance

All electrical equipment and installations should be maintained to prevent danger.

It is strongly recommended that this includes an appropriate system of visual inspection and, where necessary, testing. By concentrating on a simple, inexpensive system of looking for visible signs of damage or faults, most of the electrical risks can be controlled. This will need to be backed up by testing as necessary.

It is recommended that fixed installations are inspected and tested periodically by a competent person.

should only be tackled by people with a knowledge of the risks and the precautions needed. You must not allow work on or near exposed live parts of equipment unless it is absolutely unavoidable and suitable precautions have been taken to prevent injury, both to the workers and to anyone else who may be in the area.

Reporting of Injuries, Diseases & Dangerous Occurrences Regulations (RIDDOR)
to report work-related deaths[1], major injuries[2] or over-three-day injuries[3], work related diseases[4], and dangerous occurrences (near miss accidents)[5].

## Disability Discrimination Act

Details of disability discrimination law, with case studies to help, are found in the Disability Discrimination Act 1995 Code of Practice on Employment and Occupation [2]. This explains these legal concepts in more detail.

The three types of unlawful discrimination are:

direct discrimination; failure to make a reasonable adjustment; disability-related discrimination. 'Direct' discrimination cannot be justified and happens when:

a disabled person is treated less favourably than a non-disabled person whose relevant circumstances are the same or not materially different;  the treatment is on grounds of disability.

For example, an employer having a blanket ban on employing someone with a particular disability. Failure to make a reasonable adjustment cannot be justified and happens when an employer fails to make a reasonable adjustment [3] for a disabled person.

Disability-related discrimination is when a disabled person is treated less favourably for a disability-related reason and the treatment cannot be justified. For example, treating someone differently because they have a guide dog.

**Victimisation**

Victimisation is where someone is treated less favourably because, for instance, they have made a complaint at work or used their legal rights or have supported someone to do this.

For example, a colleague of a disabled employee attends a tribunal hearing to give evidence, in good faith, to support a disability discrimination claim. After the hearing, the employer brands the colleague 'a troublemaker' for giving evidence and withholds a bonus. This is likely to be victimisation.

**Harassment**

Harassment is any form of unwanted and unwelcome behaviour that has the purpose or effect of:

> violating the disabled person's dignity; or

> creating an intimidating, hostile, degrading, humiliating or offensive environment.

For example, a person with schizophrenia is often jokingly referred to by colleagues as being 'a bit off the wall'. People with schizophrenia may experience the world differently to most people, and this may at times affect their behaviour at work or in other settings. However, regardless of the fact that colleagues may not have intended any offence, the disabled person feels that these remarks make them nervous about the work environment. The colleagues' conduct is likely to amount to harassment and employers would have to deal with this.

Employers can help themselves by not making assumptions about disabled people and finding out about the effects of an applicant's or employee's impairment.

Help for businesses and workers on disability rights and discrimination law is also available from your local Jobcentre Plus or the EHRC.

The Department for Work and Pensions [4] has advice for employers and the EHRC [5] has particular advice for workers.

## Consumer Acts

(Consumer Protection Act 1987) The consumer has legal rights to protect them from defective products and
services. (Data Protection Act) This requires businesses that store details about clients on computer to register with the Data Protection Registrar. Even if you only store clients Names and emails for a mailing list on a computer you must still register.

## The Employment Rights Act 1996

As an employee you are entitled to ask for a written statement of the terms and conditions of your employment after you have been employed for a month. This is usually called a contract or employment terms and conditions.

The statement should include:
Details of your salary, including details of overtime payment and any commission arrangements
Usual Hours of work
Notice entitlements and obligations
Holiday entitlement
Date of commencement of employment, end date if fixed contract
Job description
Usual workplace location.

If your employer won't provide you with a written statement, then you have the right to apply to an employment tribunal who can order the employer to produce one.

## Employment Legislation

Once you have become employed, you will have certain statutory rights. These are legally binding and include the following:
A detailed pay slip showing what you have earned and what deductions have been made from your earnings

No discrimination on the basis of race, gender, sexual preference, disability, marital status or anything else

Statutory sick pay and Maternity pay

A safe working environment

At minimum of 1 week's notice of dismissal if you have been employed for at least two months

If made redundant, redundancy payment if you have been employed by the company for at least two years

The right to retain employment under the same conditions if the business is taken over by another company.

The right to complain to an industrial tribunal if you feel you have been unfairly dismissed

## The Sex Discrimination Acts 1975, 1986 and the Race Relations Act 1976

The aim of these Acts is to prevent the employer from discriminating against employees, either directly or indirectly, on the basis of their race, gender or marital status. The Equal Opportunities Commission investigates complaints of discrimination and monitors the wording of job advertisements.

## Professional framework

When you decide on a career in beauty therapy, you commit yourself to always working to the high standards set by the profession. This is the way to build your reputation as one of 'the best', gaining you the loyalty of your clients and earning you the respect of your colleagues and other professionals.

## Professional associations

It will be worth your while joining one of the professional associations which represents you and your industry. A range of services and support will be available to you including:

- technical and product updating
- business advice
- news bulletins
- special rates for insurance cover
- membership badge and display materials.

Also, you will benefit by being able to meet up regularly and speak with other professionals in the beauty industry at meetings, exhibitions and social events. Professional associations are committed to advancing beauty therapy and maintaining high standards in the profession. They provide maximum protection for the public and will work hard on your behalf. In return, you must always conduct yourself according to their **code of ethics** and maintain high standards of professional practice in all aspects of your work.

## Professional code of ethics

Each professional organisation produces its own code of practice based on expected standards of behaviour. These standards are referred to as a professional code of ethics.

A professional code of ethics is not a legal requirement but the code may be used in criminal proceedings as evidence of improper practice or negligence. Professional associations will not pay out insurance on behalf of members who breach their code of ethics.

Whichever organisation you decide to join, you will have to sign a written declaration that you will:

- always work within the law
- never treat or claim to be able to treat a medical condition
- respect client confidentiality at all times
- show respect for other professions by referring clients appropriately, for example
- to general practitioners, chiropodists, physiotherapists
- maintain high standards of hygiene and safety in all aspects of your work
- apply certain treatments only with the written permission of the client's general
- practitioner
- support, help and show loyalty to other professional beauty therapists
- never 'poach' another member's clients or criticise their work
- uphold the honour of the profession at all times, for example when working with
- clients of the opposite sex.

## Professional image

The effort you put into getting ready for work reflects your pride in the job. Clients will initially judge your professionalism on how you present yourself. You are in an industry where image and appearance are important. It is fine for you to have your own individual look provided that you appreciate that there are professional standards of dress and appearance that must be followed.

## Appearance and personal hygiene

Your appearance should reflect your professional skills and knowledge. Clients will have confidence in your abilities if you always look smart, clean and well groomed. Good personal hygiene is essential, as your work will bring you into very close contact with clients and colleagues. Good personal hygiene also helps to keep the body healthy. Here are some general rules.

## Body freshness

Have at least one bath or shower each day and use an antiperspirant.

## Uniform

Wear a clean, well-pressed overall each day. Your overall will probably be made of cotton or poly-cotton because these fabrics are easier to launder. They are also lightweight and comfortable to wear for working. Make sure your overall is not too tight. It should be loose enough for air and moisture to circulate. This helps to keep the body cool and fresh.

Your overall should also not be too short. Knee length is usually the most appropriate. Your overall should be long enough to look respectable when you sit down or if you need to stretch or lean across a client. If you wear an underskirt make sure that it does not show below your overall.

## Jewellery

Keep jewellery to the minimum. Ideally a pair of small earrings and, if you are married, a flat wedding ring. Avoid wearing bracelets, necklaces and watch straps that may get in the way during treatments or that could 'catch' the client's skin. Do not wear loose fitting chains and necklaces that could make contact with the client's skin during treatment. This is both unhygienic and uncomfortable for the client.

## Hands and feet

Keep your hands clean and smooth. Wash your hands regularly throughout the day. Breaks in the skin provide a route for bacteria. Use hand cream regularly to prevent the skin from cracking. Wear protective gloves when cleaning and when mixing chemicals. Wear correctly fitting shoes. You will spend a lot of time on your feet. Wear low-heeled shoes that are clean, smart and comfortable and appropriate for wearing with your overall. A clean pair of tights or stockings should be worn each day. They should be a natural colour, plain and not pulled or laddered. Keep a spare pair at the salon for 'emergencies'.

### Oral hygiene

Brush your teeth thoroughly after every meal as well as in the morning and last thing at night. Rinse the toothbrush well afterwards. Use dental floss regularly to remove plaque from between your teeth and under your gums. Keep a spare toothbrush at work and have a breath freshener or mouthwash on hand just in case.

### Hair care

Have clean, shiny hair dressed in a smart, manageable style. Make regular visits to the hairdresser to keep your style in shape. Long hair should be worn up or secured back off the face

.

### Make-up

A light application of make-up is all that is required to project a professional image and set a good example to clients. Refresh your make-up during the day if necessary. This can help to give you a boost when you are getting tired. A fresh application of lipstick always brightens up the face.

For more information on the health and safety aspects of your personal presentation

### Professional relationships

All sorts of relationships are developed and looked after in a professional beauty therapy environment, for example relationships between:

- staff and staff
- staff and clients

- employer and staff

  employer and clients
- the business and its suppliers
- the business and other local businesses
- the business and other organisations in the local community, for example the
- police, health services and the media.

Good professional relationships help to expand the business and build its reputation. They are built on trust, mutual respect and a sense of 'common purpose'.

(Health and Safety Executive, 2)

## CODE OF ETHICS

The Code of Ethics is provided to advise members of what is acceptable practise. It is intended to ensure that the public are protected from improper practices and to establish and maintain proper standards of behaviour by members of the Guild of Professional Beauty Therapists Limited.

The Directors of The Guild of Professional Beauty Therapists Limited reserve the right to consider any form of professional misconduct which may be brought to their attention, even though such misconduct may not appear to come within the scope or precise wording of any of the rules set out in the Code of Ethics. Applications for all categories of membership are accepted on the understanding that members will adhere to the restrictions defined in the Code of Ethics.

Applications which are made in contravention of the Code of Ethics will be considered to have been made under false pretences.

**DEFINITIONS**

'Members' refers to all categories of membership of The Guild of Professional Beauty Therapists ie. Full Members, Associate Members, Student Members and Overseas Members.

The Feminine shall include the Masculine.

# CODE OF ETHICS – Example code of ethics

Members are obliged to uphold the dignity of the profession and shall conduct themselves in conformity with good taste and professional decorum.

Members agree to act honourably towards their clients and fellow practitioners.
Members agree to maintain the confidentiality of their clients at all times.
Members must refrain from criticising the work of fellow practitioners.

Members must not undertake treatments which are beyond the scope of their professional training.   Members who do not hold a relevant medical qualification must advise clients to consult a medical practitioner in such cases.

Members must not treat any client for a condition which, to her knowledge, is at the time under the care of a medical practitioner without the knowledge and consent of that practitioner.  Members should enquire before treating a client for the first time if the client is under the care of a medical practitioner.

Members must not give injections or prescribe pills, ointments or lotions which should be prescribed by a medical practitioner.

Members must not engage in activities which are illegal or immoral.  Members must not work in, or be associated with establishments which offer services which are illegal or immoral.

## BREACH OF CODE

Any breach of The Code of Ethics may be deemed professional misconduct.  The Directors of The Guild of Professional Beauty Therapists reserve the right to suspend or terminate membership of the individual or group of individuals in such cases.  The decision of the Directors in such cases is final.

All certificates, badges, signs and publicity materials remain the property of The Guild of Professional Beauty Therapists Limited and must be returned on termination of membership.

## Insurance Providers:

**For students of Caledonian Therapy Academy, Glam Lash & MYscara :**

**1: Worldwide Alliance of Beauty Therapists www.wabt.co.uk**

**2 Balens Insurance http://www.balens.co.uk/**

**3: Guild of Beauty Therapists www.beautyguild.com**

**4: ABT Insurance http://www.abtinsurance.co.uk/**

**5: BABTAC www.babtac.com**

**For an up-to-date list of insurers contact us: Info@glamlash.co.uk**

## Links:

Glam Lash www.glamlash.co.uk

Caledonian Therapy Academy www.ctacademy.co.uk

MYscara www.myscara.co.uk

Cliodna Hair & Beauty Awards: www.cliodna.co.uk

Worldwide Alliance of Beauty Therapists www.wabt.co.uk

## Training Manual Accreditation:

# Bibliography

*Health and Safety Executive*. (2, November 2010). Retrieved from Health and Safety: http://www.hse.gov.uk

*Wikipedia*. (2010, November 3). Retrieved from http://en.wikipedia.org/wiki/Ethyl_cyanoacrylate
    Wikipedia ( 2010, November 27) Retreived from http://en.wikipedia.org/wiki/Eye_disorders

    VTCT Website ( 2010, November, 7)
    http://www.vtct.org.uk/LinkClick.aspx?fileticket=9iXgGTteHuA%3d&tabid=62
    TriLash Website (2010, November 27)
    Professional Beauty Therapy 3 - 4th Edition Lorraine Nordmann

E Doctor Online (2010, November 27) www.edoctoronline.com/medical-atlas.asp
    Vision of Joy (2010, November 27) http://www.visionsofjoy.org/images/eye%20anatomy1.jpg

Guild of Beauty Therapists (2010 November 7) www.beautyguild.com
    ABT Insurance (2010 November 27) www.abtinsurance.co.uk

Glam Lash Website (2010, November 1) www.glamlash.co.uk
Glam Lash – Manual 2009 Caledonian Therapy Academy www.ctacademy.co.uk
ITEC Standards (2010, November 10)
http://www.itecworld.co.uk/uk_qualifications/Diplomas.aspx?CategoryID=21
HABIA (2010, November 10) http://www.habia.org/index.php?page=404,404,404,1
City & Guilds (2010, November 10) http://www.cityandguilds.com/uk-qualifications.html
Consultant: Ms Margaret Welsh (Glam Lash Tutor) Margaret@ctacademy.co.uk
Consultant: Mrs Amanda Kerr (Myscara Tutor) Amanda@ctacademy.co.uk
Glam Lash – Step by Step model - Alison Cairns.